CAMBRIDGE
UNIVERSITY PRESS

CAMBRIDGE ENGLISH
Language Assessment
Part of the University of Cambridge

OFFICIAL PREPARATION MATERIAL

Cambridge English

IELTS
Life Skills

B1 Official Cambridge Test Practice

with answers

Anthony Cosgrove

Cambridge University Press
www.cambridge.org/elt

Cambridge English Language Assessment
www.cambridgeenglish.org

Information on this title: www.cambridge.org/9781316507155

© Cambridge University Press and UCLES 2016

This publication is in copyright. Subject to statutory exception
and to the provisions of relevant collective licensing agreements,
no reproduction of any part may take place without the written
permission of the publishers.

First published 2016
Reprinted 2016

Printed in Dubai by Oriental Press

A catalogue record for this publication is available from the British Library

ISBN 978-1-316-50715-5 Student's Book with answers and Audio
ISBN 978-1-316-50714-8 Audio CDs (2)

The publishers have no responsibility for the persistence or accuracy of URLs
for external or third-party internet websites referred to in this publication, and
do not guarantee that any content on such websites is, or will remain, accurate
or appropriate. Information regarding prices, travel timetables, and other factual
information given in this work is correct at the time of first printing but the
publishers do not guarantee the accuracy of such information thereafter.

CONTENTS

Information about the *IELTS Life Skills* test	4
How to use this book	5
Tips for testing learners	7
Test 1	8
Test 2	18
Test 3	28
Test 4	38
Transcripts and Answer keys	48
Prompt questions for the teacher	62
Acknowledgements	63

INFORMATION ABOUT THE *IELTS LIFE SKILLS* TEST

IELTS Life Skills is a speaking and listening test, which is available at A1 and B1 levels, as described in the *Common European Framework of Reference for Languages* (CEFR). This exam is needed to support an application to live in the United Kingdom.

The tasks in the test reflect the experience of communicating in an English-speaking country.

Two candidates take the test together, and are interviewed by one examiner. The test cannot be taken alone.

The topics covered in the test include:
- personal details and experiences
- family and friends
- buying goods
- work
- health
- leisure
- education and training
- transport
- housing
- weather.

At B1 level, candidates are expected to demonstrate that they can:
- listen and respond to spoken language, including straightforward information and narratives, and follow straightforward explanations and instructions
- communicate information, feelings and opinions on familiar topics, using appropriate formality
- talk with one or more people in a familiar situation, making relevant points and responding to what others say to reach a shared understanding about familiar topics.

Speaking tasks at B1 level may include the following skills:

- describing and comparing
- giving opinions
- giving personal information
- stating preferences
- commenting
- asking for information or descriptions
- agreeing and disagreeing
- explaining, giving reasons or justifying
- deciding
- suggesting
- selecting
- showing contrast, cause, reason or purpose
- prioritising
- planning
- persuading
- narrating
- asking about past or future events
- expressing future certainty or possibility.

What's in the test

The *IELTS Life Skills* test has four parts or 'phases':

Phase 1a *(3 minutes)*
- The examiner asks you both your name and nationality.
- The examiner gives you and your partner a topic to ask each other about
- You ask and answer each other's questions for about two minutes.
- The examiner might also ask questions, but this only happens if you stop talking early.

Phase 1b *(7 minutes)*
- The examiner asks you to speak for about 1½ minutes about a topic while the other candidate listens.
- The candidates have 1 minute to prepare what to say.
- Candidate A speaks for 1½ minutes. Candidate B then asks three questions to Candidate A, which Candidate A answers.
- Candidate B speaks for 1½ minutes. Candidate A then asks three questions to Candidate B, which Candidate B answers.

Phase 2a *(5 minutes)*
- You listen to two recordings and the examiner asks questions about what you hear. You can make notes if you want to.
- The examiner asks Candidate A one question about the first recording, and Candidate B one question about the second recording. You see the three possible answers on a page in a booklet.
- You listen to the two recordings for the second time.
- The examiner asks you two more questions. This time, the examiner asks Candidate B two questions about the first recording, and asks Candidate A two questions about the second recording.
- You listen to the two recordings again and the examiner asks each of you the same two questions.

Phase 2b *(7 minutes)*
- In the first part, the examiner asks you to plan and decide something together. For example, you are sometimes asked to imagine a situation and talk about what a friend or colleague should do.
- The examiner gives you a list of suggestions for things to talk about, and reads out this list.
- You talk together for 2 minutes. You choose an option from the list on the left, and then plan and decide what to do about it using the ideas on the right.
- In the second part, the examiner asks you to discuss a topic. This is usually connected to the plan that you talked about before.
- You talk together. If you stop talking too early, the examiner will ask a question which will help you to continue talking.

HOW TO USE THIS BOOK

For the learner

You can use this book without a teacher to prepare for the test. It is best if you can practise with another student. This can be someone else who is preparing for the *IELTS Life Skills* test, or someone who has a similar level of English to you.

The book has instructions, which make it easy to use, and audio recordings on CD and as downloadable files. You may also find it helpful to refer to the Cambridge English Language Assessment website. Here you can find sample papers from the test, including instructions for examiners: www.cambridgeenglish.org

The activities in the book are as follows:

- First, you read some test tips which give advice about each part of the *IELTS Life Skills* test.
- Then you try to do the test practice task yourself (with a partner if possible). Each task focuses on one part of the test.
- Next, you listen to an audio recording of two candidates doing the same task.

Finally, using the extra material in the book to help, you do the task for a second time.

How to use the recording

Read the information on the right page first. Then listen to two 'candidates' doing part of the test. Then you practise it with a partner or on your own.

For the listening (Phase 2a), read the questions and listen to the recording. Try to answer the questions. Then listen to the two 'candidates' answering the questions and you will hear the correct answers.

Take time to listen to each test as many times as you can. Learn any new words and language. Listen to the recording to help you say the words. Think: 'What do I need to do?' in each part of the test. The people on the recording are not real learners. They do not make mistakes with their English. Use them to help you learn. In real life, learners make mistakes in the test. You can make mistakes but you can still do well in the test. You do not need perfect English.

The best way to practise for a language test is to practise with another person. But this is not always possible. You can do the activities in the book with a partner or on your own.

For the teacher

This book is designed to give information about the *IELTS Life Skills B1* Speaking and Listening test in terms of its structure, the types of tasks used, the focus of these tasks and the interaction patterns during the test. It includes four full sample tests produced by Cambridge English Language Assessment to provide practice both in and out of the classroom.

The book takes both learner and teacher step-by-step through the test. Each sample test is supplemented with advice for learners which can be integrated into lessons. This is intended to familiarise learners with the test and to ensure they understand exactly what is expected of them in each phase. There are also:

- suggestions for useful language
- tips for what to do during the test
- ideas to help learners talk about the test topics
- recordings of model candidates doing the tests on the class CDs.

The right- and left-hand pages are designed to be used in conjunction with each other. The left-hand page follows the test format with photographs and the examiner's frame (the words the examiner speaks) for each section. You can use these with your learners to explain what happens in each part of the test. You can then use the corresponding activities on the right-hand page to help the learners practise the language and skills needed for each particular section.

A 'Tips for testing learners' section is included to help teachers prepare authentic practice tests for their learners, even if they do not have any examiner training. Practice tests provide essential, real-life exam experience, particularly for learners who may not have taken formal exams before, or whose exam experience was long ago.

The recordings and pictures will also help to show what a typical *IELTS Life Skills* test looks and sounds like at this level. You may also find it helpful to refer to the Cambridge English Language Assessment website. Here you can find sample papers from the test, including instructions for examiners: www.cambridgeenglish.org

The material in this book can be used with classes who are preparing for the *IELTS Life Skills B1* test. Students are expected to:

- attempt a task on their own without any prior input
- listen to a recording of an example answer, in which two strong candidates answer the questions
- receive some language input and/or skills development from the teacher
- attempt the task a second time.

HOW TO USE THIS BOOK

When learners are doing the test practice material, various interaction patterns are possible, including:

- whole class demonstration. The teacher plays the role of the examiner throughout, and two learners play the two candidates, with two different learners coming to the front of the class to do this for each phase. The rest of the class watch the test and feed back on their peers' performance. This could be done as follows.
  - Phase 1a with students A and B
  - Feedback on Phase 1a
  - Phase 1b with students C and D
  - Feedback on Phase 1b
  - Phase 2a with student E and F
  - Feedback on Phase 2a
  - Phase 2b with students G and H
  - Feedback on Phase 2b
- learners in groups of three with one learner playing the role of examiner. In this case, the learner who is playing the role of the examiner would need to have the exam script in front of them, and would need to be familiar with the format of the test and the task layout on the page (e.g. the use of **bold** for the examiner speaking frame)
- learners in groups of four, with three playing the roles of examiner and two candidates (as above) and the fourth being an observer. The observer watches the other three learners do a phase of the test, and then provides feedback to the learners on their performance. This is more likely to succeed if the teacher gives the observer categories to feed back on, e.g. pronunciation, accuracy of language, friendliness and politeness, etc.

TIPS FOR TESTING LEARNERS

Ideally, while preparing for the *IELTS Life Skills* test, learners should have an experience that replicates the actual exam as closely as possible, in order for them to know what to expect and be prepared. The following tips are intended to help the teacher achieve this, especially if you are holding practice speaking exams.

Setting up the room and equipment

- There should be a table and three chairs (one for the examiner and two on the other side of the table for the candidates).
- Avoid placing the candidates in front of a window where they might be dazzled by the light.
- The table should be close to a power point to plug in the CD player. Before using the material, check that the CD is working and at the right volume.
- There should be blank paper and usable pencils for the candidates to write notes during the test. In the actual test, the notes written by the candidates are treated as confidential and need to be securely destroyed. The candidates' notes are not assessed.
- The examiner should have sight of a watch or clock with a second hand, in order to time each phase and ensure that it lasts for the required amount of time. A clock should not have a noisy tick, as this may distract the students.

Conducting the tests: procedure

- The examiner reads out the instructions and questions verbatim from the examiner speaking frame.
- Other instructions to the examiner, such as when to use the candidate's name, or when to play the CD, are shown in non-bold italics.
- The examiner speaking frame is to be used verbatim. However, if a candidate does not understand something, the examiner can repeat, paraphrase or explain the task instructions. If a misunderstanding like this occurs, the candidate's mark is not affected.
- Extra questions are provided for the examiner to ask (see 'Prompt questions for the teacher' on page 62 of this book). These should only be used if the candidates run out of things to say or need a prompt. It is preferable that the candidates keep going on their own.
- During the preparation time, for example before the long turn in Phase 1b, the candidates can write notes, but do not speak to each other.

Conducting the tests: tips

- Resist jumping in too soon if candidates hesitate or stumble.
- Allow candidates a few seconds to get back on track.
- Stick to the examiner speaking frame.
- Use an appropriate speaking pace for the level but keep your voice natural and clear.
- The examiner's body language can help to reinforce the message about what the candidates are meant to do. The examiner may wish to lean in towards the candidates when addressing them. Then, in parts of the test where the candidates are expected to keep the conversation going without examiner input, the examiner may wish to withdraw slightly from the candidates, by leaning back and/or avoiding eye contact.
- Avoid making comments like 'Yes', 'Good' or 'Well done', as these can create the impression that a candidate is doing well. In the test, the examiner will say 'Thank you' when a stage of the test ends.

TEST 1

⏱ This test should not exceed 22 minutes.

Phase 1a

⏱ 3 minutes

Hello. My name is Jill.
What's your name?
Can you spell it for me?
And what shall I call you?

Where do you come from?
How long have you lived here?

My name's **Esther**.

My name's **Daniel**.

Thank you. Could I have your marksheets and identification?

Thank you.

Now you are going to ask each other some questions. I want you to find out from each other about the websites you use and why you like them. You have two minutes to talk to each other.

Thank you.

8 | TEST 1

TEST 1 PRACTICE

Test tips

- Before the exam, try to do something that helps you relax, e.g. listening to some music, or chatting with other people.
- Speak clearly. Remember that pronunciation is an important part of the Speaking test.
- When the other candidate is talking to you, show that you are interested. You could say things like 'Oh really … ?'; 'Right, … ; 'I see, that's interesting … .'

1. The examiner will ask you and the other candidate questions about your name and nationality. Look at the questions he or she will ask you and practise this part of the test with a partner.

2. Listen to the examiner ask the candidates:
   - their names
   - where they come from
   - how long they have lived here.

3. Now it's your turn. Listen and answer the examiner's questions using the same sentences you heard in the recording.

4. Working with a partner, ask each other questions about websites. Here are some questions to help you.

   Useful questions

   Which websites do you like to use?
   How often do you look at the website?
   Why do you like it?
   What kind of information are you looking for?

5. Now listen to Esther and Daniel talking to each other about the websites they like to use. As you listen, write some notes about what you hear.

6. Now it's your turn again. You and your partner ask each other questions about websites.

TEST 1

Phase 1b

⏱ 7 minutes

In this part of the test, you are each going to talk for about one and a half minutes. While you are talking, your partner will listen to you. Your partner will then ask you three questions about what you have said.

Esther, you're going to tell **Daniel** about an actor or singer you really like and why you like them.

Daniel, you're going to tell **Esther** about what your perfect home would be like and where it would be.

You both have one minute to think about what you want to say. You can make notes if you want to. If there's anything you don't understand, please ask me.

Esther, are you ready? Please tell **Daniel** about an actor or singer you really like and why you like them. **Daniel**, listen, and ask three questions at the end.

Thank you. **Daniel**, please ask **Esther** your questions now.

Thank you.

Daniel, are you ready? Please tell **Esther** about what your perfect home would be like and where it would be. **Esther**, listen, and ask three questions at the end.

Thank you. **Esther**, please ask **Daniel** your questions now.

Thank you.

TEST 1 PRACTICE

> **Test tips**
> - Listen carefully when the examiner is telling you what to talk about. Remember that you can ask the examiner if you don't understand something.
> - Before the real exam, why not practise talking for one and a half minutes on your own about a topic? You could use your mobile phone to record yourself.
> - Remember to speak slowly and clearly.

1. Listen to the examiner tell Esther and Daniel about the task. After you have listened, you are going to do the same task.

   Here are some ideas to help you:

   AN ACTOR OR SINGER I LIKE
   - Who is the person?
   - What do they look like?
   - What song / film are they most famous for?
   - Why do you like them?

   Useful language

   An *actor* / *singer* I really like is …
   He/She is most famous for …
   His/her most famous *song* / *film* is …
   I really like him/her because …

   MY PERFECT HOME
   - Where would it be?
   - Why would you like to live in this place?
   - What could you see from the window of your perfect home?
   - Who would live there with you?

   Useful language

   My perfect home would be …
   From the window, I would see …
   I would like living there because …
   I would live there with …

2. Practise this part of the test with your partner. One of you is Esther and the other is Daniel. Take turns to speak for one and a half minutes, following the examiner's instructions and using your notes to help you. Then ask each other three questions.

3. Now listen to Esther and Daniel doing this part of the test. Listen to the questions they ask each other and make some notes.

4. Now it's your turn again. Practise this part of the test with your partner.

TEST 1 | 11

TEST 1

Phase 2a

⏱ 5 minutes

In this part of the test, you are going to listen to two recordings and answer some questions. You can make notes if you want to.

You hear some students talking about parties they have been to in their college. What did they like about the parties? The music, the food or the people?

Listen to the information.

Esther, in the _first_ recording, what did they like about the parties? The music, the food or the people?

Thank you. **Daniel**, in the _second_ recording, what did they like about the parties? The music, the food or the people?

Thank you.

Now listen again, and answer these questions.

Daniel, in the _first_ recording, where in the college was the party? And what time did the party finish?

Esther, in the _second_ recording, what time did the party start? And what did the man leave at the party?

Thank you.

12 | TEST 1

TEST 1 PRACTICE

> **Test tips**
> - If you want to, you can write the questions, so that you can remember them.
> - Your notes can be in English, or in your native language.
> - You can ask the examiner to explain again if you aren't sure which question is for you, and which question is for the other candidate.
> - When you're listening, think about the meaning of the *whole* recording, not just individual words.

1. You can practise this part of the test with a partner or by yourself. If you are practising by yourself, listen and answer ALL the questions yourself.

   Look at the words on page 16. Then listen to the two recordings and answer the examiner's questions.

2. Now listen to Esther and Daniel doing this part of the test. Do they get the questions right?

TEST 1

Phase 2b

⏱ 7 minutes overall

⏱ 3 minutes

Now you're going to plan something together.

I'd like you to imagine that two of your friends are getting married and have asked for your advice about the wedding party.

First talk together about where they should have the wedding party and choose the place you think would be best.

> Where to have the party?
> • at their home
> • in a hotel
> • at a restaurant

Then plan and decide what to do about these things.

> Plan and decide
> • who they should invite
> • what food they could eat
> • what else they need to organise before the party

You have two minutes to talk about this, so don't worry if I interrupt you.

Would you like to start now?

Thank you.

⏱ 4 minutes

Now you're going to talk together about meeting people. Talk to each other about the places where you can go to meet people and the things you can do to make new friends.

Thank you. That is the end of the test.

TEST 1 PRACTICE

> **Test tips**
> - If the other candidate isn't speaking very much, ask him or her some questions.
> - Remember to work with the other candidate, and do the tasks *together*, rather than try to show that your English is better than the other candidate's.
> - Don't worry too much if you think you've made a grammar mistake. The examiner wants to hear what you can do in spoken English.
>   It's a good idea to check that the other candidate understands what you have said. To do this, you could say 'Do you see what I mean?'.

1. With a partner, listen to the examiner's instructions and look at the words on page 17. Then practise talking together. Try to keep talking for two minutes.

    Useful language

    We have to imagine that …   Shall we suggest … ?
    It depends *how / where / who* …   A *cheap / good / fun* idea would be …

2. Now listen to Esther and Daniel doing this part of the test.
   As you listen, decide whether these statements are true or false:
   a Esther checks that she has understood what the examiner has asked.
   b Esther and Daniel think the wedding celebration needs to be expensive.
   c Esther talks about her own wedding.

3. Now practise speaking again with a partner about the same topic.

4. Read the examiner's instructions on the opposite page and then practise talking together. Try to keep talking for about four minutes.

    Useful language   **Useful questions**

    Where is the best place …   How can you …
    How often do you …   Where do you go …
    What kind of people …   What's the best way to …
    What do you talk …   How easy is it to …

5. Now listen to Esther and Daniel doing this part of the test.

    Why did the examiner ask 'Is it easy or difficult to make new friends in the UK?'?

6. Now practise this part of the test again with a partner.

TEST 1 | 15

TEST 1

Visual Materials Phase 2a

What did they like about the parties?

- the music
- the food
- the people

TEST 1

Visual Materials Phase 2b

Where to have the party?
- at their home
- in a hotel
- at a restaurant

Plan and decide
- who they should invite
- what food they could eat
- what else they need to organise before the party

VISUAL MATERIALS PHASE 2B | 17

TEST 2

⏱ This test should not exceed 22 minutes.

Phase 1a

⏱ 3 minutes

Hello. My name is David.
What's your name?
Can you spell it for me?
And what shall I call you?

Where do you come from?
How long have you lived here?

My name's **Deepak**.

My name's **Li Na**.

Thank you. Could I have your marksheets and identification?

Thank you.

Now you are going to ask each other some questions. I want you to find out from each other about what kind of presents people give each other in your country and when you give them.

These can be any kind of presents, for example, for birthdays, weddings, or at festivals. You have two minutes to talk to each other.

Thank you.

TEST 2 PRACTICE

> **Test tips**
> - Learn to say the spelling of your name before the exam.
> - Be friendly and polite to the examiner.
> - Don't just give very short answers to questions, as these can sometimes sound unfriendly in English. So if the examiner asks 'How long have you lived here?', don't just say '7 years'. It would be better to say 'I moved here 7 years ago.'

1. The examiner will ask you and the other candidate questions about your name and nationality. Look at the questions he or she will ask you and practise this part of the test with a partner.

2. Listen to the examiner ask the candidates:
   - their names
   - where they come from
   - how long they have lived here.

3. Working with a partner, ask each other questions about what kind of presents people give each other in your country. Here are some questions to help you.

   Useful questions

   In your country, what kind of presents are most popular?
   What are the main occasions when people give presents in your country?
   When did you last give somebody a present?
   What present did you give?

4. Now listen to Li Na and Deepak talking to each other about what kind of presents people give each other in the candidates' own countries, and when they give them. As you listen, write some notes about what you hear.

5. Now it's your turn again. You and your partner ask each other questions about presents.

TEST 2

Phase 1b

⏱ *7 minutes*

In this part of the test, you are each going to talk for about one and a half minutes. While you are talking, your partner will listen to you. Your partner will then ask you three questions about what you have said.

Li Na, you're going to tell **Deepak** about the last time you had a meal with a group of friends. Say where you went and what you enjoyed about going there.

Deepak, you're going to tell **Li Na** about the things you always take with you when you go out and why they are important to you.

You both have one minute to think about what you want to say. You can make notes if you want to. If there's anything you don't understand, please ask me.

Li Na, are you ready? Please tell **Deepak** about the last time you had a meal with a group of friends. Say where you went and what you enjoyed about going there. **Deepak**, listen, and ask three questions at the end.

Thank you. **Deepak**, please ask **Li Na** your questions now.

Thank you.

Deepak, are you ready? Please tell **Li Na** about the things you always take with you when you go out and why they are important to you. **Li Na**, listen, and ask three questions at the end.

Thank you. **Li Na**, please ask **Deepak** your questions now.

Thank you.

TEST 2 PRACTICE

Test tips

- You have one minute to write down what you want to talk about. Don't write full sentences because there isn't time. Just write phrases or ideas.
- Try and speak accurately, but don't worry too much if you realise you've made a mistake. Try to correct it straight away.
- It's OK to ask the examiner to repeat the instruction. You could say: 'Please could you say that one more time for me? Thank you very much.'

1. Listen to the examiner tell Li Na and Deepak about the task. After you have listened, you are going to do the same task.

   Here are some ideas to help you:

   A MEAL WITH FRIENDS
   - Where did you eat?
   - Who were you with?
   - What did you have to eat?
   - What was the food like?

   Useful language

   I went for a meal *at* … / *with* …
   I ordered some …
   My friend prepared a meal of …
   The food I had was …

   THINGS YOU ALWAYS TAKE WITH YOU
   - What do you take with you?
   - Why do you need these things?
   - What do you use them for?
   - Could you manage without these things?

   Useful language

   One thing I use every day is my …
   It's very useful because it helps me to …
   I always take it with me because …
   I keep it in my *pocket* / *wallet* / *handbag*.

2. Practise this part of the test with your partner. One of you is Li Na, and the other is Deepak. Take turns to speak for one and a half minutes, following the examiner's instructions and using your notes to help you. Then ask each other three questions.

3. Now listen to Li Na and Deepak doing this part of the test and answer these questions.
   a   Who doesn't understand something?
   b   What does he or she do about it?

4. Now it's your turn again. Practise this part of the test with your partner.

TEST 2 | 21

TEST 2

Phase 2a

⏱ 5 minutes

In this part of the test, you are going to listen to two recordings and answer some questions. You can make notes if you want to.

You hear two people talking about skills they are learning. What types of lessons are they having? Driving lessons, maths lessons or computer lessons?

Listen to the information.

Li Na, in the *first* recording, what type of lessons is the man having? Driving lessons, maths lessons or computer lessons?

Thank you.

Deepak, in the *second* recording, what type of lessons is the woman having? Driving lessons, maths lessons or computer lessons?

Thank you.

Now listen again, and answer these questions.

Deepak, in the *first* recording, how many more lessons is the man going to have? And what does he like *most* about his instructor?

Li Na, in the *second* recording, why did the woman decide to do a maths course? And which day is her class?

Thank you.

TEST 2 PRACTICE

> **Test tips**
> - Listen to the examiner's questions carefully.
> - Make sure you answer the question about the right recording.
> - Don't worry if the notes that you write aren't very neat. It doesn't matter if they have spelling mistakes. The examiner doesn't mark your notes.

1. You can practise this part of the test with a partner or by yourself. If you are practising by yourself, listen and answer ALL the questions yourself.

    Look at the words on page 26. Then listen to the two recordings and answer the examiner's questions.

2. Now listen to Li Na and Deepak doing this part of the test. Do they get the questions right?

TEST 2 | 23

TEST 2

Phase 2b

⏱ 7 minutes overall

⏱ 3 minutes

Now you're going to plan something together.

I'd like you to imagine that a friend wants to start a full-time course at college, and then find a job after one year.

First talk together about which college course he should do and choose the one you think would be best.

Which college course?
- art
- science
- business

Then plan and decide what to do about these things.

Plan and decide
- how your friend should apply
- who could help him on the course
- what advice about studying you could give

You have two minutes to talk about this, so don't worry if I interrupt you.

Would you like to start now?

Thank you.

⏱ 4 minutes

Now you're going to talk together about learning new skills. Talk to each other about the type of skills you think it's useful to learn.

Thank you. That is the end of the test.

24 | TEST 2

TEST 2 PRACTICE

Test tips

- In this part of the test, you might have to imagine something. For example, that you and the other candidate already know each other, and that you both have the same friend.
- There are two sections in this part of the test. The first section (planning something together) lasts three minutes, and the second (the discussion) lasts four minutes (including the examiner's instructions), so try and keep the discussion going.
- Help the other candidate, for example if they can't remember a useful word.
- It's a good idea to start the planning task by checking that you and the other candidate understand what you have to do. You could say 'OK, shall we check that we know what we're doing? We need to … '.

1. With a partner, listen to the examiner's instructions and look at the words on page 27. Then practise talking together. Try to keep talking for two minutes.

   Useful language

   Which course …
   Do you think that our friend should …
   What do you think is the best way to …
   What advice can we …

2. Now listen to Li Na and Deepak doing this part of the test.

3. Now practise speaking again with your partner about the same topic.

4. Read the examiner's instructions on the opposite page and then practise talking together. Try to keep talking for about four minutes.

   Useful questions

   Which skills do you … ?
   Have you ever … ?
   Is it useful to … ?
   Would you like to … ?
   What skills should schools … ?

5. Now listen to Li Na and Deepak doing this part of the test.
   As you listen, decide which person, Li Na or Deepak, does the following:
   a   invites the other candidate to start talking
   b   gives an example from their own experience
   c   helps the other candidate with vocabulary

6. Now practise this part of the test again with a partner.

TEST 2 | 25

TEST 2

Visual Materials Phase 2a

What types of lessons are they having?

driving lessons

maths lessons

computer lessons

TEST 2

Visual Materials Phase 2b

Which college course?

- art
- science
- business

Plan and decide

- how your friend should apply
- who could help him on the course
- what advice about studying you could give

VISUAL MATERIALS PHASE 2B | 27

TEST 3

This test should not exceed 22 minutes.

Phase 1a

3 minutes

Hello. My name is Jill.
What's your name?
Can you spell it for me?
And what shall I call you?

Where do you come from?
How long have you lived here?

Thank you. Could I have your marksheets and identification?

Thank you.

My name's **Li Na**.

My name's **Daniel**.

Now you are going to ask each other some questions. I want you to find out from each other about a country you've visited and the countries you'd like to visit in the future. You have two minutes to talk to each other.

Thank you.

TEST 3 PRACTICE

Test tips

- At the start of the *IELTS Life Skills* test, you'll be asked about your name and nationality. If you have a short name or nickname, you can tell the examiner what it is.
- Be friendly and polite to the other candidate.
- When you're asking the other candidate questions, try and use correct grammar. This isn't a grammar test – but at this level, you should be able to ask grammatically correct questions.

1. The examiner will ask you and the other candidate questions about your name and nationality. Look at the questions he or she will ask you and practise this part of the test with a partner.

2. Listen to the examiner ask the candidates:
   - their names
   - where they come from
   - how long they have lived here.

3. Working with a partner, ask each other questions about a country you've visited and the countries you'd like to visit in the future. Here are some questions to help you.

   Useful questions

   Have you visited many countries?
   Have you been to any countries in Europe?
   When did you last visit another country?
   Which country do you really want to go to?

4. The candidates will ask each other about countries they have visited and countries they would like to visit in the future. Put the words in order to make questions.

   a visiting / which / Chinese / people / countries / do / like
   b like / would / day / you / to / visit / China / one
   c of people / lot / visit / the Philippines / do / a

5. Now listen to Li Na and Daniel talking to each other about a country they have visited and countries they would like to visit in the future. As you listen, write some notes about what you hear.

6. Now it's your turn again. You and your partner ask each other questions about countries you have visited and countries you would like to visit in the future.

TEST 3

Phase 1b

⏱ 7 minutes

In this part of the test, you are each going to talk for about one and a half minutes. While you are talking, your partner will listen to you. Your partner will then ask you three questions about what you have said.

Li Na, you're going to tell **Daniel** about something you loved doing when you were a child and why you loved doing it.

Daniel, you're going to tell **Li Na** about a time you went out with friends recently and what you did together.

You both have one minute to think about what you want to say. You can make notes if you want to. If there's anything you don't understand, please ask me.

Li Na, are you ready? Please tell **Daniel** about something you loved doing when you were a child and why you loved doing it. **Daniel**, listen, and ask three questions at the end.

Thank you. **Daniel**, please ask **Li Na** your questions now.

Thank you.

Daniel, are you ready? Please tell **Li Na** about a time you went out with friends recently and what you did together. **Li Na**, listen, and ask three questions at the end.

Thank you. **Li Na**, please ask **Daniel** your questions now.

Thank you.

TEST 3 PRACTICE

Test tips

- Some people find it difficult talking for this long, but you'll find it gets much easier with practice.
- When the examiner says 'Thank you', that means it's time for you to stop talking.
- If you are Candidate B, remember that you must listen to Candidate A when he or she is speaking. Don't try to use their speaking as extra time to prepare more, as this might seem rude.
- While the other candidate is speaking, think of three questions you would like to ask, and note them down on paper.

1. Listen to the examiner tell Li Na and Daniel about the task. After you have listened, you are going to do the same task.

   Here are some ideas to help you:

   SOMETHING I LOVED DOING WHEN I WAS A CHILD AND WHY I LOVED DOING IT
   - the age when you started the activity
   - who you did the activity with
   - why you enjoyed this activity
   - whether you still do this activity

   Useful language

   I'd like to tell you about …
   I really enjoyed … –ing
   I remember that …
   For me, …
   I thought it was …

   A TIME WITH FRIENDS AND WHAT WE DID TOGETHER
   - where you went
   - who you went with
   - how you got there
   - what you did there

   Useful language

   I'm going to talk about …
   Some friends and I …
   It was a … day
   The best part was …

2. Practise this part of the test with your partner. One of you is Li Na and the other is Daniel. Take turns to speak for one and a half minutes, following the examiner's instructions and using your notes to help you. Then ask each other three questions.

3. Now listen to Li Na and Daniel doing this part of the test. Listen to their conversation, and note how they use the **Useful language** above.

4. Now it's your turn again. Practise this part of the test with your partner, and try to use the phrases in **Useful language** above.

TEST 3 | 31

TEST 3

Phase 2a

⏱ 5 minutes

In this part of the test, you are going to listen to two recordings and answer some questions. You can make notes if you want to.

You hear two people giving students information about different things. Who is speaking? A careers advisor, a teacher or a student?

Listen to the information.

Li Na, in the *first* recording, who is speaking? A careers advisor, a teacher or a student?

Thank you.

Daniel, in the *second* recording, who is speaking? A careers advisor, a teacher or a student?

Thank you.

Now listen again, and answer these questions.

Daniel, in the *first* recording, where is the careers advisor's office? And what should the students take with them to the talk?

Li Na, in the *second* recording, how much is a travel card for students? And where can the students buy a travel card?

Thank you.

32 | TEST 3

TEST 3 PRACTICE

> **Test tips**
> - You only need to know the answer to your questions. You don't need to know the answer to the other candidate's questions.
> - The examiner will ask you a question about the first recording, and then two questions about the second recording. Make sure you know if your question is about the first recording or the second recording.
> - You can ask the examiner to repeat the question if you didn't hear it properly or if you don't understand it.
> - Listen carefully to the whole recording, even if you think you already know the answer to your question.

1. You can practise this part of the test with a partner or by yourself. If you are practising by yourself, listen and answer ALL the questions yourself.

    Look at the words on page 36. Then listen to the two recordings and answer the examiner's questions.

2. Now listen to Li Na and Daniel doing this part of the test and answer the questions.
    a Do they answer the questions correctly?
    b Who was confused about what to do in the test?
    c What did he/she do about it?
    d Will this affect his/her score?

TEST 3 | 33

TEST 3

Phase 2b

⏱ 7 minutes overall

⏱ 3 minutes

Now you're going to plan something together.

I'd like you to imagine that a friend is trying to decide which job to do in the future. He needs some advice about which job to choose.

First talk together about who he should ask for advice about jobs and choose the one you think would be best.

> Who to ask for advice?
> - friends
> - family
> - teachers

Then plan and decide what to do about these things.

> Plan and decide
> - what qualifications or experience to get
> - where to look for work
> - what advice to give someone starting a new job

You have two minutes to talk about this, so don't worry if I interrupt you.

Thank you.

⏱ 4 minutes

Now you're going to talk about getting information. Talk to each other about how you get the information you need in day-to-day life, for example, about studying or about shops and services.

Thank you. That is the end of the test.

34 | TEST 3

TEST 3 PRACTICE

> **Test tips**
> - Make sure you understand the examiner's instructions. Ask if you're not sure.
> - React to what the other candidate says. You could say 'I see what you mean'; 'That's a good idea'; 'Oh yes, good point'; 'Yes, I suppose so'.
> - If you don't understand what the other candidate said, you can ask them to repeat or explain something. You could say 'So, are you saying that … ?'; 'What do you mean exactly?'; 'Sorry, I don't get it'.

1. With a partner, listen to the examiner's instructions and look at the words on page 37. Then practise talking together. Try to keep talking for two minutes.

   Useful language

   Can I just check something?   Good point.
   Would you like to start?   Sorry, I don't get it.
   Not really.   That's a good question
   I suppose so.

2. Now listen to Li Na and Daniel doing this part of the test. Which candidate (Li Na or Daniel) does the following:
   a asks the examiner to explain something?
   b invites the other candidate to speak first?
   c disagrees with the other candidate?
   d suggests talking about the next part of the task?

3. Now practise speaking with a partner about the same topic.

4. Read the examiner's instructions on the opposite page and then practise talking together. Try to keep talking for about four minutes.

   Useful questions

   What's the best way to find out about … ?   Apart from the internet, how can you … ?
   Is it better to … or to … ?   How useful are libraries to … ?

5. Now listen to Li Na and Daniel doing this part of the test and answer the questions.
   a How did Li Na check the price of the fridge?
   b What does Daniel think the internet is good for?
   c What is the best way of finding out how good something is?

6. Now practise this part of the test again with a partner.

TEST 3 | 35

TEST 3

Visual Materials Phase 2a

Who is speaking?

- a careers advisor
- a teacher
- a student

TEST 3

Visual Materials Phase 2b

Who to ask for advice?
- friends
- family
- teachers

Plan and decide
- what qualifications or experience to get
- where to look for work
- what advice to give someone starting a new job

VISUAL MATERIALS PHASE 2B | 37

TEST 4

This test should not exceed 22 minutes.

Phase 1a

⏱ 3 minutes

Hello. My name is David.
What's your name?
Can you spell it for me?
And what shall I call you?

Where do you come from?
How long have you lived here?

My name's **Esther**.

My name's **Deepak**.

Thank you. Could I have your marksheets and identification?

Thank you.

Now you are going to ask each other some questions. I want you to find out from each other about the places you have to go to in town, for example, post offices and banks, and what you need to do there. You have two minutes to talk to each other.

Thank you.

38 | TEST 4

TEST 4 PRACTICE

Test tips

- Make eye contact with the examiner when you are introducing yourself, and from time to time during the test.
- You can ask the examiner to repeat anything you don't understand. You could say 'I'm sorry, could you say that again, please?' or 'Could you repeat that, please?'.
- You'll take the test with one other candidate, who you may not know, so before the test starts, chat with him/her in English while you are waiting.
- When the examiner says 'Thank you', that means it's time for you to stop talking.
- When you ask the other candidate some questions, try to make the conversation as friendly as possible.

1. The examiner will ask you and the other candidate questions about your name and nationality. Look at the questions he or she will ask you and practise this part of the test with a partner.

2. Listen to the examiner ask the candidates:
   - their names
   - where they come from
   - how long they have lived here.

3. Working with a partner, ask each other questions about places that you go to in town (like post offices and banks). Here are some questions to help you.

   Useful questions
   How often do you go to the bank / post office, … ?
   What kind of things do you do there?
   How often do you go into town?
   What do you like about doing things in town?

4. Now listen to Esther and Deepak talking to each other about doing things in town. As you listen, write some notes about what you hear.

5. Now it's your turn again. You and your partner ask each other questions about places you go to in town.

TEST 4 | 39

TEST 4

Phase 1b

⏱ 7 minutes

In this part of the test, you are each going to talk for about one and a half minutes. While you are talking, your partner will listen to you. Your partner will then ask you three questions about what you have said.

Esther, you're going to tell **Deepak** about a time you helped someone and how you helped them.

Deepak, you're going to tell **Esther** about the kind of music you like and when you listen to it.

You both have one minute to think about what you want to say. You can make notes if you want to. If there's anything you don't understand, please ask me.

Esther, are you ready? Please tell **Deepak** about a time you helped someone and how you helped them. **Deepak**, listen, and ask three questions at the end.

Thank you. **Deepak**, please ask **Esther** your questions now.

Thank you.

Deepak, are you ready? Please tell **Esther** about the kind of music you like and when you listen to it. **Esther**, listen, and ask three questions at the end.

Thank you. **Esther**, please ask **Deepak** your questions now.

Thank you.

TEST 4 PRACTICE

Test tips

- Remember to pause as you speak. This makes it easier for you to think of what to say, and it makes it easier for others to understand you.
- Think of three questions to ask about what your partner says in his or her presentation.
- When you ask questions, try to link them to what they have just said. You could say 'You said that you … , so I wanted to ask you if …'; 'I was interested that you said … '; 'But don't you think that … ?'.
- Try to vary the vocabulary and grammar in your questions. Your questions could start with 'When / How often / Why / Do you / Is it / Have you ever … '.

1. Listen to the examiner tell Esther and Deepak about the task. After you have listened, you are going to do the same task.

   Here are some ideas to help you:

   A TIME WHEN YOU HELPED SOMEONE
   - Who did you help?
   - Where were you?
   - Why did the person need help?
   - How did you help them?
   - What happened afterwards?

   Useful language
   This happened when …
   … needed help …
   … asked if I could …
   I offered to …

   MUSIC YOU LIKE
   - Who's your favourite singer / band?
   - What is their best song?
   - When do you listen to this music?
   - Do you go to concerts?
   - Do you have any CDs of this music?

   Useful language
   … favourite kind of music …
   … a song called …
   … makes me feel …
   … a *band / singer / song* I really like is …
   I first heard …
   You should listen to …

2. Practise this part of the test with your partner. One of you is Esther and the other is Deepak. Take turns to speak for one and a half minutes, following the examiner's instructions and using your notes to help you. Then ask each other three questions.

3. Now listen to Esther and Deepak doing this part of the test. Listen to their conversation and answer the question. Who says the following: Deepak or Esther?
   a Actually …
   b Anyway …
   c As you probably know …
   d What about …
   e I think …
   f I'm going to tell you about …
   g In fact …
   h I really like …

4. Now it's your turn again. Practise this part of the test with your partner.

TEST 4 | 41

TEST 4

Phase 2a

⏱ *5 minutes*

In this part of the test, you are going to listen to two recordings and answer some questions. You can make notes if you want to.

You hear two students talking about the jobs they would like to do. What jobs would they like to do? Dentist, actor or teacher?

Listen to the information.

Esther, in the <u>first</u> recording, what job would the student like to do? Dentist, actor or teacher?

Thank you.

Deepak, in the <u>second</u> recording, what job would the student like to do? Dentist, actor or teacher?

Thank you.

Now listen again, and answer these questions.

Deepak, in the <u>first</u> recording, who wants the student to do this work? And what is she planning to do next year?

Esther, in the <u>second</u> recording, how do the student's parents feel about the job he wants to do? And where does he want to work in the future?

Thank you.

TEST 4 PRACTICE

Test tips

- Remember that you hear both recordings twice, and that you'll be asked questions about each recording.
- Remember: first, you have to answer *one* question about one recording. Then you have to answer *two* questions about the second recording.
- In the exam, don't try to answer the questions that the other candidate needs to answer.
- When you write down your questions, it's OK to just write the important words. You don't need to write every word.
- When you're listening to the recording, it's a good idea to write down the answer to your question as soon as you hear it. This will help you to remember the answer when you are asked to say it.

1. You can practise this part of the test with a partner or by yourself. If you are practising by yourself, listen and answer ALL the questions yourself.

    Look at the words on page 46. Then listen to the two recordings and answer the examiner's questions.

2. Now listen to Esther and Deepak doing this part of the test. What is the order in which they are asked the questions?

TEST 4

Phase 2b

⏱ 7 minutes overall

⏱ 3 minutes

Now you're going to plan something together.

I'd like you to imagine that a friend is going to have an interview for a job as a packer in a local factory.

First talk together about what he should wear at the interview and choose the one you think would be best.

> **What should he wear?**
> - a suit and tie
> - a shirt and smart trousers
> - casual clothes

Then plan and decide what to do about these things.

> **Plan and decide**
> - what questions he could ask
> - how he should behave
> - how else he should prepare for the interview

Would you like to start now?

Thank you.

⏱ 4 minutes

Now you're going to talk together about starting a new job. Talk to each other about what is enjoyable and what can be difficult about starting a new job.

Thank you. That is the end of the test.

44 | TEST 4

TEST 4 PRACTICE

> **Test tips**
> - If you don't agree with the other candidate, it's OK to say that you disagree. But it's important that you do this in a polite and friendly way. You could say 'Actually, I've got a different idea'; 'Well, I'm not so sure about that'; 'I'm not sure that's the best idea'.
> - Try to speak accurately, but don't worry if you think you've made a mistake. It's a test of speaking, not grammar!
> - When the examiner says 'Thank you', that means it's time for you to stop talking.

1. With a partner, listen to the examiner's instructions and look at the words on page 47. Then practise talking together. Try to keep talking for two minutes.

    Useful language

    … look smart   … look serious
    … turn up for work   … the best thing to wear
    … go for his interview … make a good impression

2. Now listen to Esther and Deepak doing this part of the test. Listen and write down what they say when they disagree with each other.

3. Now practise speaking again with a partner about the same topic.

4. Read the examiner's instructions on the opposite page and then practise talking together. Try to keep talking for about four minutes.

    Useful questions

    On your first day of a new job, what should you … ?
    Have you started a … ?
    What can be enjoyable when you … ?
    What can be difficult when you … ?
    What's the best way to … ?

5. Now listen to Esther and Deepak doing this part of the test. What enjoyable things and what difficulties do they mention?

6. Now practise this part of the test again with a partner.

TEST 4

Visual Materials Phase 2a

What jobs would they like to do?

dentist

actor

teacher

46 | VISUAL MATERIALS PHASE 2A

TEST 4

Visual Materials Phase 2b

What should he wear?

- a suit and tie
- a shirt and smart trousers
- casual clothes

Plan and decide

- what questions he could ask
- how he should behave
- how else he should prepare for the interview

VISUAL MATERIALS PHASE 2B | 47

TRANSCRIPTS AND ANSWER KEYS

Test 1 Transcript (CD1)

🎧 02 Test 1, Phase 1a

Examiner:	Hello. My name is Jill. What's your name?
Esther:	My name's Esther.
Examiner:	Can you spell it for me?
Esther:	Yes, of course. It's E–S–T–H–E–R.
Examiner:	And what's your name?
Daniel:	My name's Daniel.
Examiner:	Can you spell it for me?
Daniel:	Sure: D–A–N–I–E–L.
Examiner:	Where do you come from, Esther?
Esther:	I'm from Nigeria.
Examiner:	How long have you lived here?
Esther:	I think it's about three years now, yes, nearly three years.
Examiner:	Daniel, where do you come from?
Daniel:	I come from Cebu in the Philippines.
Examiner:	And how long have you lived here?
Daniel:	For about a year now.
Examiner:	Thank you. Could I have your marksheets and identification? Thank you.

🎧 03

Now you answer the examiner's questions.

Examiner:	Hello. My name is Jill. What's your name?

[Pause for reply]

Examiner:	Can you spell it for me?

[Pause for reply]

Examiner:	Where do you come from?

[Pause for reply]

Examiner:	How long have you lived here?

[Pause for reply]

Examiner:	Thank you.

🎧 04

Examiner:	Now you are going to ask each other some questions. I want you to find out from each other about the websites you use and why you like them. You have two minutes to talk to each other.
Daniel:	OK, Esther, do you like using the internet?
Esther:	Oh, yes, very much. Every day, when I get home from work, I always use the internet – to find information and to check my email. But what I like most is Facebook.
Daniel:	Is that for keeping in touch with friends?
Esther:	Yes, for keeping in touch with my family in Nigeria. It's really good because I can still feel close to them, and it's much cheaper than an air ticket!
Daniel:	And do you use Skype sometimes?
Esther:	Yes, sometimes I use Skype at the weekend, when I want to have a long conversation with my sister. How about you, Daniel? Which websites do you like?
Daniel:	Well, I really like sport, so there are quite a few sport websites I look at, especially basketball.
Esther:	I see. Is basketball popular in the Philippines?
Daniel:	Oh yes, very. And the team I used to play for in Cebu has quite a good website.
Esther:	And do you watch matches online?
Daniel:	Yes, I can see bits of their games.
Esther:	Oh, right. Do you ever see people that you know?
Daniel:	Yes, I love watching some of my friends, especially when they play really well.
Examiner:	Thank you.

🎧 05 Test 1, Phase 1b

Examiner:	In this part of the test, you are each going to talk for about one and a half minutes. While you are talking, your partner will listen to you. Your partner will then ask you three questions about what you have said. Esther, you're going to tell Daniel about an actor or singer you really like and why you like them. Daniel, you're going to tell Esther about what your perfect home would be like and where it would be. You both have one minute to think about what you want to say. You can make notes if you want to. If there's anything you don't understand, please ask me.

🎧 06

Examiner:	Esther, are you ready? Please tell Daniel about an actor or singer you really like and why you like them. Daniel, listen, and ask three questions at the end.
Esther:	OK … one actor I've always liked is Daniel Craig. You probably know him if you've seen his James Bond films … like *Skyfall*. That's what he's most famous for. For me, he's the best James Bond, even better than Sean Connery. But he's been in lots of other films too – some thrillers, and films about war and history too. What I like most about him is his face, especially his eyes when he acts. When you look at him, you don't know what he's thinking. When I'm watching a film with him in, and he's on screen, I always look at him, even when someone else is talking. I think he's a really brilliant actor.
Examiner:	Thank you. Daniel, please ask Esther your questions now.
Daniel:	Have you seen any other films with Daniel Craig?
Esther:	One or two, yes. I think *The Golden Compass* is really good.
Daniel:	And who do you think will be the next James Bond?
Esther:	Oh, I have no idea! But I don't think anybody will be as good as Daniel Craig.
Daniel:	If you could meet Daniel Craig, what would you say to him?
Esther:	Well, maybe I'd ask if he is married! Or perhaps I'd just ask for his autograph!
Examiner:	Thank you.

[pause]

TRANSCRIPTS AND ANSWER KEYS

Examiner: Daniel, are you ready? Please tell Esther about what your perfect home would be like and where it would be. Esther, listen, and ask three questions at the end.

Daniel: OK … the place I'd like to tell you about is in the Philippines. It's close to my home town of Cebu. Cebu is quite a big city, and I like to get away at weekends to an island called Bohol. That's the place where I'd really like to live. The reason I chose Bohol is that it's really peaceful. It has beautiful scenery, as well as some great beaches. The food is good, and I've got lots of cousins and friends who live there. One place I really love there is a group of hills called the Chocolate Hills. Maybe one day I'd like to build a house there, a modern house where I could sit and look at the sea when I'm eating breakfast – that would be really relaxing!

Examiner: Thank you. Esther, please ask Daniel your questions now.

Esther: So Daniel, how close is this island to your city?

Daniel: You have to take a boat, and it's a couple of hours.

Esther: Why are they called the Chocolate Hills?

Daniel: In the summer, the grass on the hills gets dry and goes brown, so all these little hills look like bits of chocolate!

Esther: Really? That's interesting. And my last question is about your home. What kind of home would you like to have?

Daniel: Well, in the future, if I have enough money, I'd like to build a big house for my family with three bedrooms and a swimming pool ... oh, and a view of the sea.

Examiner: Thank you.

🎧 07 Test 1, Phase 2a

Listen and answer the examiner's questions.

Examiner: In this part of the test, you are going to listen to two recordings and answer some questions. You can make notes if you want to.
You hear some students talking about parties they have been to in their college. What did they like about the parties? The music, the food, or the people? Listen to the information.

Recording 1.
Male: Hi Sonia. Did you go to that party on Monday?
Female: Yes, I got there in the end – I thought it was going to be in the Art Department so I went there first, but they held it in the Science Building – it took me ages to find.
Male: Oh. Anyway, what was it like?
Female: It was really good because some of my friends were there. And I met some other students who were very nice too.
Male: Sounds good!

Female: Yes, and it was lovely chatting with the teachers. The only thing was, the music was very loud, but apart from that, it was very enjoyable. It actually went on until after midnight and I stayed until the end, though I wasn't going to.

Recording 2.
Female: Did you get to the opening of the college gym on time yesterday?
Male: Yes. I got there at six but it didn't actually begin until seven.
Female: What was it like?
Male: Well, the gym looks great. And there were some very nice things to eat but I didn't know any of the students or staff there, so I didn't really talk to anyone.
Female: Oh, that's a shame. Well, at least they fed you well.
Male: True. The students brought in typical dishes from their countries, which were great. The only problem is, I put my coursebook down under a chair and then forgot all about it. I'll have to go back later today and see if it's still there.

Examiner: Learner A, in the *first* recording, what did they like about the parties? The music, the food or the people?
[Pause for reply]
Thank you.
Examiner: Learner B, in the *second* recording, what did they like about the parties? The music, the food or the people?
[Pause for reply]
Examiner: Thank you.
Now listen again, and answer these questions.
Learner B, in the *first* recording, where in the college was the party?
And what time did the party finish?
Learner A, in the *second* recording, what time did the party start?
And what did the man leave at the party?
[You will hear Recording 1 and Recording 2 again.]
Examiner: Learner B, in the *first* recording, where in the college was the party?
[Pause for reply]
Examiner: And what time did the party finish?
[Pause for reply]
Examiner: Learner A, in the *second* recording, what time did the party start?
[Pause for reply]
Examiner: And what did the man leave at the party?
[Pause for reply]
Examiner: Thank you.

TRANSCRIPTS AND ANSWER KEYS

🎧 08

Now listen to Esther and Daniel doing this part of the test.

Examiner: In this part of the test, you are going to listen to two recordings and answer some questions. You can make notes if you want to.
You hear some students talking about parties they have been to in their college. What did they like about the parties? The music, the food or the people?
Listen to the information.

[The recordings are repeated.]

Examiner: Esther, in the *first* recording, what did they like about the parties? The music, the food or the people?
Esther: The people.
Examiner: Thank you. Daniel, in the *second* recording, what did they like about the parties? The music, the food or the people?
Daniel: It was the food.
Examiner: Now listen again, and answer these questions.
Daniel, in the *first* recording, where in the college was the party? And what time did the party finish?
Esther, in the *second* recording, what time did the party start? And what did the man leave at the party?

[The recordings are repeated.]

Examiner: Daniel, in the *first* recording, where in the college was the party?
Daniel: It was in the Science Building.
Examiner: And what time did the party finish?
Daniel: It finished after midnight.
Examiner: Esther, in the *second* recording, what time did the party start?
Esther: It didn't start until 7 o'clock.
Examiner: And what did the man leave at the party?
Esther: He left his coursebook there.
Examiner: Thank you.

🎧 09 **Test 1, Phase 2b**

Examiner: Now you're going to plan something together. I'd like you to imagine that two of your friends are getting married and have asked for your advice about the wedding party. First talk together about where they should have the wedding party and choose the place you think would be best: at their home; in a hotel; at a restaurant.
Then plan and decide what to do about these things: who they should invite; what food they could eat; what else they need to organise before the party.
You have two minutes to talk about this, so don't worry if I interrupt you.

🎧 10

Esther: OK, so we have to imagine that our two friends are getting married. Is that right?
Daniel: Yes, that's it.

Esther: OK, well it depends how many people they want to invite.
Daniel: … and how much money they want to spend!
Esther: Sure. Well, I don't think our friends want to spend very much, do they? I mean, a lot of people spend lots and lots of money on a wedding.
Daniel: They do … but I don't think you have to.
Shall we suggest a wedding for them that's going to be really cheap, so not in a hotel or a restaurant and then our friends can decide if they like our idea?
Esther: OK. So I suppose a really cheap idea would be a party at their home or something like a picnic in the park!
Daniel: Yes, why not? It could be fun. And because it won't be so expensive for each person, they could invite as many people as they want.
Esther: When I got married, we didn't invite many people because we didn't want to spend too much.
Examiner: Thank you.

🎧 11

Examiner: Now you're going to talk together about meeting people. Talk to each other about the places where you can go to meet people and the things you can do to make new friends.
Esther: OK, well, shall we start with places we go to meet friends?
Daniel: Alright. So, Esther, where do you usually go to meet friends?
Esther: Oh, lots of places. I go to my college, to an English class. And the other students, my classmates, are my friends. So we have a chat at college, usually in the café after lessons. How about you?
Daniel: Also a café, actually. Quite near where I live there's a café where a lot of the Filipino expats …
Esther: Expats? What do you mean?
Daniel: People who used to live in another country. So I'm a Filipino expat living in the UK, you know.
Esther: Did you know all of these people before you came to Britain?
Daniel: No, I met a couple of other people from Cebu when I was over here, and they told me about this café. So I started going. And I met lots of really nice people there.
Esther: So the place where you go to meet up with your friends is also the place where you go to make new friends?
Daniel: Exactly. And this café is quite well known in the Filipino community here. So, normally, when someone arrives in the UK from the Philippines, quite soon they hear about this café and go there too. So we get to know them as well. How about you?
Esther: Well, I suppose these days I meet a lot of people online. I use social networks a lot, and it's a great way to get to know your friends' friends.

50 | TRANSCRIPTS AND ANSWER KEYS

TRANSCRIPTS AND ANSWER KEYS

Examiner:	Is it easy or difficult to make new friends in the UK?
Daniel:	I've met quite a few of my neighbours. Most of them are British. And we say hello to each other on the street. What about you?
Esther:	Well, through my work, I've got to know quite a few people. I work in a big shop, and lots of my colleagues are British. We get on really well, and some of them have a great sense of humour.
Examiner:	Thank you. That is the end of the test.

Test 1 Answer Key

Phase 2a

1.

Learner A: *What did they like about the parties?* the people
Learner B: *What did they like about the parties?* the food

Learner B: *Where in the college was the party?* (in) (the) Science Building / Department
What time did the party finish? (after) midnight
Learner A: *What time did the party start?* (at) 7 (o'clock)
What did the man leave at the party? (his) (course) book

2. Yes

Phase 2b

2. a True **b** False **c** True

5. Because Esther and Daniel had stopped talking, and the examiner wanted them to continue.

Test 2 Transcript (CD1)

🎧 12 Test 2, Phase 1a

Examiner:	Hello. My name is David. What's your name?
Li Na:	It's Li Na.
Examiner:	Li Na? Can you spell it for me?
Li Na:	Yes, of course. It's L–I–N–A.
Examiner:	And what's your name?
Deepak:	My name's Deepak.
Examiner:	Deepak? Can you spell it for me?
Deepak:	Yes, it's D–E–E–P–A–K.
Examiner:	Li Na, where do you come from?
Li Na:	I come from Wuhan in China.
Examiner:	And how long have you lived here?
Li Na:	Not very long, actually. It's about 6 months now.
Examiner:	Where do you come from, Deepak?
Deepak:	My family are from Punjab, in northern India.
Examiner:	And how long have you lived here?
Deepak:	I moved here 7 years ago.
Examiner:	Thank you. Could I have your marksheets and identification? Thank you.

🎧 13

Examiner:	Now you are going to ask each other some questions. I want you to find out from each other about what kind of presents people give each other in your country and when you give them. These can be any kind of presents, for example, for birthdays, weddings, or at festivals. You have two minutes to talk to each other.
Li Na:	Right, so in India, do people give each other a lot of presents?
Deepak:	Well it depends. Sometimes, yes. And sometimes presents can be very expensive, like when there's a wedding. Sometimes the bride's family actually give a car to her new husband's family.
Li Na:	Wow! That's a really expensive present.
Deepak:	Well, yes, but I don't think that happens very often. It's more usual to just give something like chocolates or flowers if you're invited to someone's home.
Li Na:	A bit like in the UK!
Deepak:	Yes. When you go to someone's home, do you bring them something like that?
Li Na:	Yes, flowers or chocolates. Or sometimes something to drink or eat.
Deepak:	Lovely. How about in China – which occasions are the biggest celebrations?
Li Na:	Well, birthdays are celebrated more and more these days, like in other countries. But older people's birthdays are more important, especially when someone is over seventy-five.
Deepak:	What sort of things do people often give each other?
Li Na:	Lots of things, for example, herbal medicines are a popular gift for older people.
Examiner:	Thank you.

🎧 14 Test 2, Phase 1b

| Examiner: | In this part of the test, you are each going to talk for about one and a half minutes. While you are talking, your partner will listen to you. Your partner will then ask you three questions about what you have said. Li Na, you're going to tell Deepak about the last time you had a meal with a group of friends. Say where you went and what you enjoyed about going there. Deepak, you're going to tell Li Na about the things you always take with you when you go out and why they are important to you.
You both have one minute to think about what you want to say. You can make notes if you want to. If there's anything you don't understand, please ask me. |
|---|---|

TRANSCRIPTS AND ANSWER KEYS

🎧 15

Deepak: Sorry, can I just check something?
Examiner: Yes, of course.
Deepak: Do we discuss the topics together, or speak on our own, like a presentation?
Examiner: You both speak on your own.
Deepak: OK, thanks. Sorry, I wanted to make sure.
Examiner: So, now you have one minute to think about what you want to say.
Examiner: Li Na, are you ready? Please tell Deepak about the last time you had a meal with a group of friends. Say where you went and what you enjoyed about going there. Deepak, listen, and ask three questions at the end.
Li Na: Right, the last time I had a meal with a group of friends was actually last night, because I share a flat with four other girls in the city centre. We're all from different countries, and we take turns to cook. So we often eat Chinese, Thai, Hungarian, Libyan and Portuguese food, because those are my flatmates' nationalities. Last night, my flatmate wasn't able to cook because she had to stay late at work. And the rest of us didn't really want to cook either, so we decided to go out and have fish and chips. There's a takeaway just around the corner from us, so we went there and bought some chips and ate them in the park, because it was a nice evening.
Examiner: Thank you, Li Na. Deepak, please ask Li Na your questions now.
Deepak: Li Na, you said the takeaway is close to your home, so do you go there often?
Li Na: No – actually, it was the first time.
Deepak: OK, and did you like the fish and chips? Did they taste good?
Li Na: Yes, but it was quite salty, so I wouldn't eat it every day.
Deepak: And my last question is about your friend. Was she really working late, or did she just not want to cook?
Li Na: That's a good question. No, I'm sure she was really working late.
Examiner: Deepak, are you ready? Please tell Li Na about the things you always take with you when you go out and why they are important to you. Li Na, listen, and ask three questions at the end.
Deepak: I'd like to tell you about the most important thing that I take around with me. It's my wallet, and all the documents inside it, especially my bank card, because I pay for almost everything with it. I don't have much cash with me, and I use my debit card for payments, even for small things, like just getting a sandwich for lunch or something like that. My wallet also contains my driving licence, and I drive a lot, so I always have that too. I also have my keys – house keys, car keys and keys to my office.

Examiner: Thank you, Deepak. Li Na, please ask Deepak your questions now.
Li Na: OK. Deepak, you said you have a debit card. Do you also have a credit card?
Deepak: No, I don't. Credit cards just mean that you can spend money you haven't got, so I don't think it's a good idea to have one.
Li Na: When you pay for things with a bank card, do you ever have a problem because the shop only wants cash?
Deepak: Sometimes, yes, especially in small shops – that does happen, yes. So I always have a little bit of cash with me.
Li Na: And you said you always have your driving licence with you. Is that because you have to have your driving licence with you when you drive?
Deepak: That's a good question. I don't really know, but I suppose the answer is probably yes.
Examiner: Thank you.

🎧 16 **Test 2, Phase 2a**

Listen and answer the examiner's questions.

Examiner: In this part of the test, you are going to listen to two recordings and answer some questions. You can make notes if you want to.
You hear two people talking about skills they are learning. What types of lessons are they having? Driving lessons, maths lessons, or computer lessons? Listen to the information.

Recording 1.
Male: It's going really well. I've had eight lessons now – and I plan to have another three. They do make a big difference. Parking used to be so difficult for me but now I'm much more confident about it. It's going to be really useful to have my licence. I'll be able to pick up the children from their maths club after school. But the best thing is, it's going to be much less hard work doing the weekly shop – no more worrying about having the right change for the bus fare. I must say, I'm lucky. I'd really recommend the man who's teaching me – he's very patient. So, if you want to try …

Recording 2.
Female: Well, I've always been interested in the subject, but just not very good at it. I'm OK with addition and subtraction and things like that, but anything more difficult, like fractions, I can't do very well at all. I finally made the decision to do it so I could help the children with their homework. I attend one evening a week. It's convenient because my husband can babysit on a Thursday while I go – and he does a computer course on a Wednesday, so it works out really well. Next year, I'm hoping to do the next level which includes algebra. I'm looking forward to it but I just hope it's not too difficult.

TRANSCRIPTS AND ANSWER KEYS

Examiner: Learner A, in the *first* recording, what type of lessons is the man having? Driving lessons, maths lessons or computer lessons?

[Pause for reply]

Examiner: Thank you. Learner B, in the *second* recording, what type of lessons is the woman having? Driving lessons, maths lessons or computer lessons?

[Pause for reply]

Examiner: Thank you.
Now listen again, and answer these questions.
Learner B, in the *first* recording, how many more lessons is the man going to have?
And what does he like most about his instructor?
Learner A, in the *second* recording, why did the woman decide to do a maths course?
And which day is her class?

[You will hear Recording 1 and Recording 2 again.]

Examiner: Learner B, in the *first* recording, how many more lessons is the man going to have?

[Pause for reply]

Examiner: And what does he like most about his instructor?

[Pause for reply]

Examiner: Learner A, in the *second* recording, why did the woman decide to do a maths course?

[Pause for reply]

Examiner: And which day is her class?

[Pause for reply]

Examiner: Thank you.

🎧 17

Now listen to Li Na and Deepak doing this part of the test.

Examiner: In this part of the test, you are going to listen to two recordings and answer some questions. You can make notes if you want to.
You hear two people talking about skills they are learning. What types of lessons are they having? Driving lessons, maths lessons or computer lessons? Listen to the information.

[The recordings are repeated.]

Examiner: Li Na, in the *first* recording, what type of lessons is the man having? Driving lessons, maths lessons or computer lessons?

Li Na: Driving lessons.

Examiner: Thank you. Deepak, in the second recording, what type of lessons is the woman having? Driving lessons, maths lessons or computer lessons?

Deepak: I think she said she's learning maths.

Examiner: Thank you. Now listen again, and answer these questions.
Deepak, in the *first* recording, how many more lessons is the man going to have? And what does he like most about his instructor?
Li Na, in the *second* recording, why did the woman decide to do a maths course? And which day is her class?

[The recordings are repeated.]

Examiner: Deepak, in the *first* recording, how many more lessons is the man going to have?

Deepak: He's going to have another three lessons.

Examiner: And what does he like most about his instructor?

Deepak: He's very patient.

Examiner: Thank you. Li Na, in the *second* recording, why did the woman decide to do a maths course?

Li Na: So she could help her kids with their maths homework.

Examiner: And which day is her class?

Li Na: It's on Thursdays.

Examiner: Thank you.

🎧 18 **Test 2, Phase 2b**

Examiner: Now you're going to plan something together. I'd like you to imagine that a friend wants to start a full-time course at college, and then find a job after one year. First talk together about which college course he should do and choose the one you think would be best: art; science; business.
Then plan and decide what to do about these things: how your friend should apply; who could help him on the course; what advice about studying you could give. You have two minutes to talk about this, so don't worry if I interrupt you.

🎧 19

Deepak: So, if he wants to get a job after the course, he should study something practical shouldn't he?

Li Na: Yes, so I don't think art would be very useful.

Deepak: No, I'm afraid I agree. It's fun to paint, but it probably isn't going to earn him any money, is it!

Li Na: Probably not. And science is only possible if he already knows enough about science. I think I would choose a business course.

Deepak: Me too. That'll give him a good chance of finding a job. So, shall we decide how he should apply?

Li Na: Yes. I think he should look at two or three different colleges first, and decide which one he likes.

Deepak: Yes, he could also go and meet the teachers before he chooses which college to study at.

Li Na: Yes, that's a good idea. Because they'll be helping him on the course. Not just in the classes, but they'll help him with his studies; they'll show him how to write essays.

Deepak: Sure.

Li Na: So, could you give him any advice about studying?

Deepak: I'd say: be organised. Do your work as early as you can, not as late as you can.

Examiner: Thank you.

TRANSCRIPTS AND ANSWER KEYS | 53

TRANSCRIPTS AND ANSWER KEYS

🎧 20

Examiner:	Now you're going to talk together about learning new skills. Talk to each other about the type of skills you think it's useful to learn.
Li Na:	OK. Deepak, would you like to start? What kind of skills do you think it's useful to learn?
Deepak:	That's a good question. Well, these days, it's always good to have IT skills, isn't it? In fact, it's quite difficult to get a job without these skills.
Li Na:	Yes, definitely. But the thing is that a lot of people think 'Oh, I can use a computer, I don't need to learn anything else'. But that's not true, because there's always something else you can learn.
Deepak:	New computer programs, that sort of thing?
Li Na:	Exactly. Even when you can do something OK, you can always learn to do it better.
Deepak:	Yes, I agree. If you want to succeed in your life, you should always try to keep learning. That's what my grandmother always said to me!
Li Na:	And not just in your job but also in the things you enjoy doing at home.
Deepak:	What sort of things do you mean?
Li Na:	Well, for example, in my spare time I like to do photography. And I can do basic editing, like making a picture lighter or darker, with the free software that came with my computer.
Deepak:	Right. Was it difficult to learn?
Li Na:	No, not really, but I wanted to do it better, so I started learning how to use some software that I had to pay for, software that is more …
Deepak:	… sophisticated?
Li Na:	Sophisticated, exactly. You can do more things, and do them better.
Deepak:	Right. And did you need to know about this programme for work, or just for fun?
Li Na:	Just for fun really. What about you?
Deepak:	Well, I think it's also important to learn new skills that can help us in our jobs.
Li Na:	Yes, and help us get a better job in the future. What new skills have you learned in your job?
Deepak:	At work, we can go on training courses to help us improve the service to our customers.
Examiner:	Thank you. That is the end of the test.

Test 2 Answer Key (CD2)

Phase 1b

3.
a Deepak
b He politely interrupts the examiner saying: 'Sorry, can I just check something?' He then asks whether he and Li Na need to talk together or on their own.

Phase 2a

1.
Learner A: *What types of lessons are they having?* driving (lessons)
Learner B: *What types of lessons are they having?* maths (lessons)

Learner B: *How many more lessons is the man going to have?* 3
What does he like most about his instructor? he's (very) patient
Learner A: *Why did the woman decide to do a maths course?* (so she could)/(to) help the children with their homework
Which day is her class? (on) Thursday(s)

2. Yes

Phase 2b

5. **a** Li Na   **b** Li Na   **c** Deepak

Test 3 Transcript (CD2)

🎧 02 Test 3, Phase 1a

Examiner:	Hello. My name is Jill. What's your name?
Li Na:	My name's Li Na.
Examiner:	Can you spell it for me?
Li Na:	Yes, it's L–I–N–A.
Examiner:	And what is your name?
Daniel:	I'm Daniel.
Examiner:	Can you spell it for me?
Daniel:	Sure: D–A–N–I–E–L.
Examiner:	Where do you come from, Daniel?
Daniel:	I'm from the Philippines.
Examiner:	And how long have you lived here?
Daniel:	I arrived in the UK a year ago.
Examiner:	Where do you come from, Li Na?
Li Na:	I'm from China.
Examiner:	And how long have you lived here?
Li Na:	About half a year now.
Examiner:	Thank you. Could I have your marksheets and identification? Thank you.

🎧 03

Examiner:	Now you are going to ask each other some questions. I want you to find out from each other about a country you've visited and the countries you'd like to visit in the future. You have two minutes to talk to each other.
Li Na:	Would you like to start, Daniel?
Daniel:	OK. Well Li Na, have you visited many countries?
Li Na:	Not very many. I went on holiday to Italy with my family two years ago.
Daniel:	Oh, Italy, I'd like to go there.
Li Na:	Have you been to any other countries in Europe?
Daniel:	Not yet, no. I've only been in Britain for a year you see, so I haven't had much time.
Li Na:	Which country do you really want to go to?
Daniel:	Maybe Spain, because I've heard it's really beautiful. Which countries do Chinese people like to visit?

54 | TRANSCRIPTS AND ANSWER KEYS

TRANSCRIPTS AND ANSWER KEYS

Li Na:	That's a good question. I've heard that the Maldives is really popular, especially for people going on holiday … and France – especially Paris. Would you like to visit China one day, Daniel?
Daniel:	Maybe, yes, why not? I'm sure it's very different to the Philippines.
Li Na:	Do a lot of people visit the Philippines?
Daniel:	You mean from other countries? Yes, I don't know how many, but a lot come from Europe and other places. They like visiting some of the islands, like Boracay.
Examiner:	Thank you.

🎧 04 Test 3, Phase 1b

Examiner:	In this part of the test, you are each going to talk for about one and a half minutes. While you are talking, your partner will listen to you. Your partner will then ask you three questions about what you have said. Li Na, you're going to tell Daniel about something you loved doing when you were a child and why you loved doing it. Daniel, you're going to tell Li Na about a time you went out with friends recently and what you did together. You both have one minute to think about what you want to say. You can make notes if you want to. If there's anything you don't understand, please ask me.

🎧 05

Examiner:	Li Na, are you ready? Please tell Daniel about something you loved doing when you were a child and why you loved doing it. Daniel, listen, and ask three questions at the end.
Li Na:	OK, well, I'd like to tell you about playing tennis. I started playing when I was really young – about three, I think. My dad took me to lessons at the local university. There was a really good sports centre there, and they had classes for children starting from three. I really enjoyed going there because it was a big adventure. I remember that the lessons were in a huge sports hall with eight tennis courts. For me, it was my first time in such a big space, and I thought it was really exciting. And the coach, she was really good. She was good at tennis, and she was good with children, because there were always lots of fun things to do, like learning to hold the racket, hit a ball over the net, and that sort of thing.
Examiner:	Thank you. Daniel, please ask Li Na your questions now.
Daniel:	You said you were three when you started. Isn't that too young?
Li Na:	No, I don't think so. If you start something when you're young, then you have lots of time to get better and better.
Daniel:	How many children were in the group with you?
Li Na:	Not very many, I think there were about twenty.
Daniel:	Do you still play tennis, now?
Li Na:	Yes, I used to play when I was in China, but I haven't played here in England yet. Perhaps I will soon.
Examiner:	Thank you. Daniel, are you ready? Please tell Li Na about a time you went out with friends recently and what you did together. Li Na, listen, and ask three questions at the end.
Daniel:	I'm going to talk about a day out that I had recently. Some friends and I went to Bath for a day. Bath is in the west of England, near to Bristol. It's a small city, with lots of old buildings, and it gets quite a lot of tourists. My friend wanted to go and see it, so he took three of us in his car. We left early – at about seven in the morning, because we didn't know how long the journey takes. But it was only about two hours, so it wasn't too bad. It was a fantastic day because we visited the Abbey, some of the old buildings and we looked at the shops. The best part was the lunch – it was a beautiful, warm, sunny day, so we bought some food and ate it in a park. It was a great day out.
Examiner:	Thank you. Li Na, please ask Daniel your questions now.
Li Na:	Was it easy to get to Bath from London?
Daniel:	Yes, you can take the motorway most of the way – it goes quite close to Bath.
Li Na:	What were the shops like?
Daniel:	Well, I don't really like shops. My friend wanted to look at the shops but I didn't really want to. To be honest, I think the shops there are exactly the same as the shops everywhere else.
Li Na:	You said you had lunch outside. What did you have to eat?
Daniel:	We bought a Chinese takeaway. It was delicious!
Examiner:	Thank you.

🎧 06 Test 3, Phase 2a

Listen and answer the examiner's questions.

Examiner:	In this part of the test, you are going to listen to two recordings and answer some questions. You can make notes if you want to. You hear two people giving students information about different things. Who is speaking? A careers advisor, a teacher or a student? Listen to the information.

Recording 1.

Female:	Most of you are doing part-time courses here and you may be thinking about getting an evening or weekend job. Well, the best thing to do is go and see Mr Davis. He'll give you advice about applying for jobs you're interested in. And you'll find him in the small office next to the library. He's giving a talk for new students at three thirty today in Room B7. Now I know your lessons with me finish at four normally but I don't

TRANSCRIPTS AND ANSWER KEYS | 55

mind if you leave class early if you'd like to hear what he has to say. All you'll need if you go is a pen and paper to take a few notes – and I'm sure you'll find his talk very helpful.

Recording 2.

Male: Well, our teacher has asked me to talk to you today about getting to college because I've been studying here for a year already. If you have lessons every day of the week like me then the best way to travel here is by bus and what you need to get is a travel card. They'd normally cost eight pounds fifty a week but for us, they're much cheaper – only four pounds fifty, so they're very good value unless, of course, you live near the college and can walk here. If you live further away, you can get these cards from the newsagent's next to the college. But don't forget to take a photograph with you when you buy your first one.

Examiner: Learner A, in the *first* recording, who is speaking? A careers advisor, a teacher or a student?

[Pause for reply]

Examiner: Thank you. Learner B, in the *second* recording, who is speaking? A careers advisor, a teacher or a student?

[Pause for reply]

Examiner: Thank you.
Now listen again, and answer these questions.
Learner B, in the *first* recording, where is the careers advisor's office? And what should the students take with them to the talk?
Learner A, in the *second* recording, how much is a travel card for students?
And where can the students buy a travel card?

[You will hear Recording 1 and Recording 2 again.]

Examiner: Learner B, in the *first* recording, where is the careers advisor's office?

[Pause for reply]

Examiner: And what should the students take with them to the talk?

[Pause for reply]

Examiner: Learner A, in the *second* recording, how much is a travel card for students?

[Pause for reply]

Examiner: And where can the students buy a travel card?

[Pause for reply]

Examiner: Thank you.

🎧 07

Now listen to Li Na and Daniel doing this part of the test.

Examiner: In this part of the test, you are going to listen to two recordings and answer some questions. You can make notes if you want to.
You hear two people giving students information about different things. Who is speaking? A careers advisor, a teacher or a student?
Listen to the information.

[The recordings are repeated.]

Examiner: Li Na, in the *first* recording, who is speaking? A careers advisor, a teacher or a student?
Li Na: I think it was a teacher.
Examiner: Thank you. Daniel, in the second recording, who is speaking? A careers advisor, a teacher or a student?
Daniel: A student was speaking.
Examiner: Now listen again, and answer these questions.
Daniel, in the *first* recording, where is the careers advisor's office? And what should the students take with them to the talk?
Li Na, in the *second* recording, how much is a travel card for students? And where can the students buy a travel card?
Li Na: Oh, my questions are about the *second* recording now, not the first one, like before?
Examiner: That's right.
Li Na: Oh, of course, I got confused. Sorry, could you repeat my questions please?
Examiner: Yes of course. Li Na, in the *second* recording, how much is a travel card for students? And where can the students buy a travel card?
Li Na: Thank you.

[The recordings are repeated]

Examiner: Daniel, in the *first* recording, where is the careers advisor's office?
Daniel: It's next to the library.
Examiner: And what should the students take with them to the talk?
Daniel: Just a pen and paper.
Examiner: Li Na, in the *second* recording, how much is a travel card for students?
Li Na: For students it's four pounds fifty.
Examiner: And where can the students buy a travel card?
Li Na: From the newsagent's next to the college.
Examiner: Thank you.

🎧 08 **Test 3, Phase 2b**

Examiner: Now you're going to plan something together. I'd like you to imagine that a friend is trying to decide which job to do in the future. He needs some advice about which job to choose.
First talk together about who he should ask for advice about jobs and choose the one you think would be best: friends; family; teachers.
Then plan and decide what to do about these things: what qualifications or experience to get; where to look for work; what advice to give someone starting a new job.
You have two minutes to talk about this, so don't worry if I interrupt you.

TRANSCRIPTS AND ANSWER KEYS

09

Examiner:	Would you like to start now?
Li Na:	Sorry, can I just check something?
Examiner:	Yes, of course.
Li Na:	Are we supposed to imagine that *we* want to choose a job?
Examiner:	No, not you – a *friend*. A friend wants to choose a job, and he needs advice from you and Daniel.
Li Na:	I see, thank you. Sorry, I wasn't sure.
Examiner:	It's fine to ask.
Li Na:	Daniel, would you like to start?
Daniel:	OK. So, our friend wants to choose a career. It's probably the most important decision he'll make in his life.
Li Na:	The most important? Not really. I mean, if he starts a job and then doesn't like it, he can just change it.
Daniel:	But that can be expensive. That's why I think he should ask as many people as possible.
Li Na:	Is that what you did?
Daniel:	Yes. When I was 14 or 15, I asked lots of people for advice.
Li Na:	Even kids who were the same age as you?
Daniel:	Yes. It's good to ask friends.
Li Na:	Yes, I suppose so.
Daniel:	We also need to think about these three other things, don't we?
Li Na:	Oh yes, good point.
Daniel:	The first thing is qualifications. It depends, doesn't it? Some jobs need lots of qualifications, others don't.
Li Na:	Sorry, I don't get it. Are you saying qualifications aren't important?
Daniel:	No, not exactly. I mean that not everybody needs qualifications. If you're a photographer, you don't need a degree in photography. You just need to take really good pictures.
Li Na:	Yes, I suppose you're right.
Examiner:	Thank you.

10

Examiner:	Now you're going to talk about getting information. Talk to each other about how you get the information you need in day-to-day life, for example, about studying or about shops and services.
Daniel:	Can I just check something?
Examiner:	Yes, of course.
Daniel:	We need to discuss how we find out things. Is that right?
Examiner:	Exactly. You need to talk to each other about how you get the information you need in day-to-day life, for example, about studying or about shops and services.
Li Na:	So, if we need information, like what's on at the cinema or what the English homework is, that kind of thing, where do we get the information from?
Daniel:	Oh, I see. Thanks. Well, I suppose the obvious answer is from our phones. I mean, if you need to know a train time, or an address, or what's the best way to get somewhere by public transport. All that information is so easy, as long as your phone is charged, and the internet signal is OK. What do you think, Li Na?
Li Na:	Yes, I agree with you. I don't know what I'd do without my phone. One thing I use my phone for is checking the prices of things. My flatmates and I needed a new fridge last month, and I could compare the prices and find the cheapest place to buy it.
Daniel:	And did you buy it?
Li Na:	Yes, and I saved about fifty pounds!
Examiner:	Do you think the internet is always the best way to find out information?
Daniel:	Almost always. It's great if you just want facts – prices, times, addresses, that kind of thing.
Li Na:	That's true. But if you want to know how *good* something is, the internet isn't always so good.
Daniel:	Yes, I agree. I wanted to buy a motorbike a few years ago. I was interested in one particular motorbike. And I thought 'I'll look online, and see how good it is'.
Li Na:	Like, if it's reliable, if it can go a long way without using lots of fuel, that sort of thing?
Daniel:	Exactly.
Li Na:	And was it easy to find that sort of information?
Daniel:	Not really. I did an internet search for that motorbike, but all I got was advertising and marketing. Everything said, you know, this motorbike is really cool.
Li Na:	Ha!
Daniel:	Just adverts! Telling me to buy the motorbike. But nothing about why I should buy it.
Li Na:	Yes, I think that's typical isn't it. Most of the internet is just advertising. But if you want to know more, it's not always so good. The best way to get information about how good something is to ask people.
Daniel:	That's what I did in the end. I asked a couple of people who own motorbikes what they thought about the one I wanted to buy.
Examiner:	Thank you. That is the end of the test.

TRANSCRIPTS AND ANSWER KEYS

Test 3 Answer Key

Phase 1a

4.
a Which countries do Chinese people like visiting?
b Would you like to visit China one day?
c Do a lot of people visit the Phillipines?

Phase 2a

1.
Learner A: *Who is speaking?* a teacher
Learner B: *Who is speaking?* a student

Learner B: *Where is the careers advisor's office?* next (to) (the) library
What should students take with them to the talk? (a) pen and paper
Learner A: *How much is a travel card for students?*
4 (pounds) 50 (pence/p)
Where can the students buy the travel card? (the) newsagent's (next to the college)

2.
a Yes
b Li Na
c She asked the examiner to repeat her question.
d No

Phase 2b

2. **a** Li Na **b** Li Na **c** Daniel **d** Daniel
5. **a** She used her phone. **b** checking facts **c** asking people

Test 4 Transcript (CD2)

🎧 11 Test 4, Phase 1a

Examiner:	Hello. My name is David. What's your name?
Esther:	I'm Esther.
Examiner:	Can you spell it for me?
Esther:	Yes, of course. It's E–S–T–H–E–R.
Examiner:	And what's your name?
Deepak:	My name's Deepak.
Examiner:	And can you spell it for me?
Deepak:	Sure: D double-E-P-A-K.
Examiner:	Where do you come from, Esther?
Esther:	I'm from Nigeria.
Examiner:	And how long have you lived here?
Esther:	I've been here for three years now.
Examiner:	Deepak, where do you come from?
Deepak:	I come from India.
Examiner:	And how long have you lived here?
Deepak:	For about seven years now.
Examiner:	Thank you. Could I have your marksheets and identification? Thank you.

🎧 12

Examiner:	Now you are going to ask each other some questions. I want you to find out from each other about the places you have to go to in town, for example, post offices and banks, and what you need to do there. You have two minutes to talk to each other.
Esther:	OK. Do you often go into town, Deepak?
Deepak:	Quite often, yes, if I've got things to do. But I only go if I have to, because it takes up too much time. Like going to the bank. I usually just check my bank balance online.
Esther:	Yeah, me too. Some things take too much time! Like going to the post office. Sometimes I send things to my family in Nigeria, so I go to the post office for that. Occasionally it's really busy and I have to wait for ages. I don't really like that.
Deepak:	Sure. How often do you go to the post office?
Esther:	Maybe about once a month. How about you?
Deepak:	I go less often. But I have to go to the post collection place sometimes.
Esther:	Oh yes, when the postman tried to deliver something, but you were out. And they leave a little card.
Deepak:	Yes, exactly. I think the postman only comes when I'm out, actually! What about shopping – do you often go into town to go shopping?
Esther:	Well, not into the town centre. But there's a big shopping centre near my home, so I go there.
Deepak:	What do you like about going there?
Esther:	Everything's in the same place. There's a huge supermarket, and some other big shops there. And parking is easy – and free!
Examiner:	Thank you.

🎧 13 Test 4, Phase 1b

Examiner:	In this part of the test, you are each going to talk for about one and a half minutes. While you are talking, your partner will listen to you. Your partner will then ask you three questions about what you have said. Esther you're going to tell Deepak about a time you helped someone and how you helped them. Deepak, you're going to tell Esther about the kind of music you like and when you listen to it. You both have one minute to think about what you want to say. You can make notes if you want to. If there's anything you don't understand, please ask me.

🎧 14

Examiner:	Esther, are you ready? Please tell Deepak about a time you helped someone and how you helped them. Deepak, listen, and ask three questions at the end.
Esther:	I'm going to tell you about a time when I helped someone. In fact, it happened this morning while I was coming to college to do this test. The college is on a busy road. I was waiting to cross the road at the traffic lights and there was an old lady next to me.

TRANSCRIPTS AND ANSWER KEYS

	She was looking in her bag for something, maybe looking for her phone or something. But she actually dropped her purse, so some of her coins came out and were just on the ground by my feet. I picked the coins up and gave them back to her. And I helped her pick up some other things too from the ground. Anyway, I was glad I was able to help her.
Examiner:	Thank you. Deepak, please ask Esther your questions now.
Deepak:	What about the other people – what did they do?
Esther:	They didn't really do anything. I don't think anyone else noticed the lady dropping stuff. It was very noisy, with all the traffic.
Deepak:	How much money did you pick up?
Esther:	I don't know exactly. I think there was a pound coin, and a few other coins.
Deepak:	And what did the lady say to you?
Esther:	Oh, she was very nice. She said 'Thank you.' And then I think she said 'That's very kind of you.'
Examiner:	Thank you. Deepak, are you ready? Please tell Esther about the kind of music you like and when you listen to it. Esther, listen, and ask three questions at the end.
Deepak:	I like a lot of different kinds of music: pop, rock, lots of different things. As you probably know, Indian films are famous. And like most Indian people, I really like movies, and the music from Bollywood films. When I was living in India, I went to the cinema a lot, probably every week, to see the latest films. And I think almost every Bollywood film has songs and dancing – it's a very important part of the film. And a lot of people learn the songs and the words to all the songs. When I was younger, I used to try and learn the dances too, but I don't do that any more!
Examiner:	Thank you, Deepak. Esther, please ask Deepak your questions now.
Esther:	You talked about Indian films. I think I heard you say *Bollywood*? Is that right? What is Bollywood?
Deepak:	That's a good question. Well, the American film industry is called Hollywood, so they made a word for the Indian film industry that sounds nearly the same: Bollywood. It starts with a 'B' because a lot of the films were made in Mumbai, and the old name for Mumbai is Bombay. So Bombay plus Hollywood makes Bollywood!
Esther:	Ah, I see. Thank you. And are the songs in English?
Deepak:	Not generally, no. The films – and the songs – are usually in Hindi.
Esther:	I don't know any Bollywood music, but I'd like to hear some. Can you recommend a song?
Deepak:	Well, there are so many. You could search online for *Lagaan*. It's a film. But all the songs from that are brilliant. I think you will like it!
Esther:	Thanks. I'll try that.
Examiner:	Thank you.

🎧 15 Test 4, Phase 2a

Listen and answer the examiner's questions.

Examiner:	In this part of the test, you are going to listen to two recordings and answer some questions. You can make notes if you want to. You hear two students talking about the jobs they would like to do. What jobs would they like to do? Dentist, actor or teacher? Listen to the information. *Recording 1.*
Female:	Until quite recently, I wanted to study medicine or maybe dentistry when I got older. Then, last year in a play at school, I played the part of an old woman, which was difficult for me, but I had a fantastic time. I loved performing in front of the audience and now I've decided that I'd like to do that kind of thing again. My dad thinks it's great and would really like me to try but my mum hates the idea. She says jobs like that are just not serious. But I've decided that when this year's over, I'm going to go to drama school. It's my life and I want to do a job I enjoy. *Recording 2.*
Male:	People often look surprised when I tell them what job I'd like to have. Most of my friends want to go into teaching and they say things like 'Do you really want to spend your life looking inside people's mouths?' or 'Do you like the idea of looking at teeth all day?' But I've talked to my mum and dad and they're quite pleased about it. Most of all, I want to help people who get frightened when they come for a filling. I'd be good at that. I'd love to get a job in another country. When I was growing up, I lived in Spain and I loved the sun. So, maybe I'll think about that and …
Examiner:	Learner A, in the *first* recording, what job would the student like to do? Dentist, actor or teacher?
[Pause for reply]	
Examiner:	Thank you. Learner B, in the *second* recording, what job would the student like to do? Dentist, actor or teacher?
[Pause for reply]	
Examiner:	Thank you.
[Pause for reply]	
	Now listen again, and answer these questions. Learner B, in the *first* recording, who wants the student to do this work? And what is she planning to do next year? Learner A in the *second* recording, how do the student's parents feel about the job he wants to do? And where does he want to work in the future?
[You will hear Recording 1 and Recording 2 again.]	

TRANSCRIPTS AND ANSWER KEYS | 59

TRANSCRIPTS AND ANSWER KEYS

Examiner: Learner B, in the *first* recording, who wants the student to do this work?
[Pause for reply]
Examiner: And what is she planning to do next year?
[Pause for reply]
Examiner: Learner A, in the *second* recording, how do the student's parents feel about the job he wants to do?
[Pause for reply]
Examiner: And where does he want to work in the future?
[Pause for reply]
Examiner: Thank you.

🎧 16

Now listen to Esther and Deepak doing this part of the test.

Examiner: In this part of the test, you are going to listen to two recordings and answer some questions. You can make notes if you want to.
You hear two students talking about the jobs they would like to do.
What jobs would they like to do? Dentist, actor or teacher?
Listen to the information.
[The recordings are repeated.]
Examiner: Esther, in the first recording, what job would the student like to do? Dentist, actor or teacher?
Esther: She wants to be an actor.
Examiner: Deepak, in the second recording, what job would the student like to do? Dentist, actor or teacher?
Esther: He'd like to be a dentist.
Examiner: Now listen again, and answer these questions.
Deepak, in the *first* recording, who wants the student to do this work? And what is she planning to do next year? Esther, in the *second* recording, how do the student's parents feel about the job he wants to do? And where does he want to work in the future?
[The recordings are repeated]
Examiner: Deepak, in the *first* recording, who wants the student to do this work?
Deepak: Her dad.
Examiner: And what is she planning to do next year?
Deepak: I think she wants to go to drama school.
Examiner: Esther, in the *second* recording, how do the student's parents feel about the job he wants to do?
Esther: They're pleased about it.
Examiner: And where does he want to work in the future?
Esther: In another country.
Examiner: Thank you.

🎧 17 **Test 4, Phase 2b**

Examiner: Now you're going to plan something together. I'd like you to imagine that a friend is going to have an interview for a job as a packer in a local factory. First talk together about what he should wear at the interview and choose the one you think would be best: a suit and tie; a shirt and smart trousers; casual clothes.
Then plan and decide what to do about these things: what questions he could ask; how he should behave; how else he should prepare for the interview. You have two minutes to talk about this, so don't worry if I interrupt you.

🎧 18

Examiner: Would you like to start now?
Deepak: OK, so we need to decide what he should wear for his interview.
Esther: Yes, it's a job in a factory isn't it?
Deepak: Yes.
Esther: So I don't think he needs to be smart. Factory workers don't wear suits, do they? So they don't need smart clothes at their interviews.
Deepak: Well, I'm not so sure about that, Esther. Factory workers probably have to wear uniforms to work. But they don't wear uniforms to their interview, do they?
Esther: I don't think it matters.
Deepak: What do you think he should wear?
Esther: Well, like I say, if you have an interview for a job in an office, you wear a suit. But that doesn't mean everyone has to wear a suit for every interview. It depends on the job. I think he can just wear casual clothes.
Deepak: What, like jeans?
Esther: Yes, if he wants. Why not?
Deepak: I'm not convinced that's the best idea.
Esther: What clothes do you suggest?
Deepak: Actually, I've got a different idea. I think he should be smart. He should look serious, to show he is a serious worker.
Esther: I don't think we're going to agree! But never mind – let's also think about what else he should do.
Deepak: Before the interview, I think he should find out about the job and the company.
Esther: Yes, I agree. And he can think of questions to ask about the company too, because you can usually ask questions in interviews, can't you?
Examiner: Thank you.

🎧 19

Examiner: Now you're going to talk together about starting a new job. Talk to each other about what is enjoyable and what can be difficult about starting a new job.
Deepak: Well, I think the main thing is that when you've got a new job, you're really pleased that you've got it.
Esther: Yes, and it's nice that you can get to know a new group of people – your new colleagues. And then, if you're getting paid more than you were before, it's nice to see the extra money arriving in your bank account each month!

TRANSCRIPTS AND ANSWER KEYS

Deepak: And another thing – if your new job is different to your old one, then it can be quite interesting, getting used to it.

Esther: Doing new things, you mean? Yes, I suppose so.

Deepak: And what about the other question? What kind of things can be difficult?

Esther: I think it depends on the job. My sister recently started a job at a call centre, answering phone calls, and that was really difficult. The callers wanted to know lots of stuff about their computer system, and they wanted her to fix their problems. It's all very technical, and my sister had to learn a lot of this technical stuff in a very short time.

Deepak: And is she enjoying it more now?

Esther: No, not really. The customers only call her when they have a problem, so they're sometimes already quite annoyed when they call her.

Deepak: But it's not *her* fault that their computer system isn't working properly!

Esther: Exactly. But some people think it is. And that makes her job more difficult.

Examiner: How important is it to get on with your colleagues in a new job?

Deepak: Oh, I think it's really important. Perhaps the most important thing. It helps you enjoy the job when you're with a nice group of people, even if the work is boring. You can still enjoy it if you like the team of people you're with.

Esther: I agree. But you've sometimes got to make an effort when you start to get to know people, especially if English isn't your first language, and you have to try hard to get to know people, and to understand everything people are saying. When I got my first job in England in the supermarket, it was very difficult because my manager spoke so quickly and I worried about making mistakes. But my colleagues were very nice and always helped me if I didn't know how to do something. Now some of them are my best friends and, of course, I am much more confident when I am at work.

Examiner: Thank you. That is the end of the test.

Test 4 Answer Key

Phase 1b

3.

a Esther
b Esther
c Deepak
d Deepak
e Deepak
f Esther
g Esther
h Deepak

Phase 2a

1.

Learner A: *What job would the student like to do?* (an) actor / (an) actress / acting / work on stage

Learner B: *What job would the student like to do?* (a) dentist

Learner B: *Who wants the student to do this work?* (her) dad/father
What is she planning to do next year? (go to) drama school

Learner A: *How do the student's parents feel about the job he wants to do?* (they're) (quite) pleased (about it)
Where does he want to work in the future? (in) another country

2.

One question for Esther; one question for Deepak; two questions for Deepak; two questions for Esther

Phase 2b

2.

I'm not so sure about that …
But that doesn't mean …
I'm not convinced that's the best idea …
I don't think we're going to agree …

5.

enjoyable things: pleased to get a job; meet new people; extra money

difficulties: learning about technology; difficult customers; speaking in English

PROMPT QUESTIONS FOR THE TEACHER

These questions are taken from the test paper. They are suggested questions the examiner can use to encourage candidates to speak more.

Test 1, Phase 1a
Which website do you use most often? (Why?)
Do you think using the internet can help you to learn English? (Why?/Why not?)
How long do you spend each day using the internet? Do you think that's too long? (Why?/Why not?)
Do you think the internet is the best place to find information? (Why?/Why not?)

Test 1, Phase 2b
Is it easy or difficult to make new friends in (*candidate's town or city*)?
When was the last time you made a new friend? (Where did you meet?)
Do you think it's a good idea to make new friends online? (Why?/Why not?)
Do you think your friends always have to share the same interests as you? (Why?/Why not?)

Test 2, Phase 1a
Do you enjoy shopping for presents for people? (Why?/Why not?)
What was the best present you ever received? (Why?)
What was the best present you ever gave? (Why?)
What do you think are good presents for children? (Why?)

Test 2, Phase 2b
Do you think it's important to keep learning new skills after leaving school? (Why?/Why not?)
Do you think children learn new skills more quickly than adults? (Why?/Why not?)
What skills do people in your country need in order to get a good job?
Is there a new skill that you would like to learn? (Why would you like to learn to do that?)

Test 3, Phase 1a
What's the best thing about this country? (Why?)
What do you think is the best way to travel to other countries? (Why?)
If you could visit any country in the world, where would you go? (Why?)
What advice would you give someone about moving to live in another country? (Why?)

Test 3, Phase 2b
How do you find information about things to do in (*candidate's town or city*)?
Do you often use a library? (What do you use it for?)
Do you think the internet is always the best way to find out information? (Why?/Why not?)
Some people think we won't need books and magazines in the future because we can read everything online. What do you think?

Test 4, Phase 1a
How often do you go into the town/city centre? (What do you usually do there?)
Do you find it easy or difficult to use places like post offices and banks? (Why?)
Do you use the internet for banking or post office services instead of going into town? (Why?/Why not?)
Have you ever been to the library in (*candidate's town or city*)? Is it a good library? (What can you do there?)

Test 4, Phase 2b
What's the most difficult thing about starting a new job? (Why?)
Should people always ask lots of questions when they're starting a new job? (Why?/Why not?)
How important is it to get on with your colleagues in a new job? (Why?)
Do you remember starting your last job? (Tell me about it.) (How did you feel?)

ACKNOWLEDGEMENTS

Cover illustration by Andy Potts (Anna Goodson Illustration Agency) using photographs by Gareth Boden (taken on commission for Cambridge University Press).

The photographs on pages 8–14, 18–24, 28–34, 38–44. were taken on commission by Gareth Boden for Cambridge University Press.

Recordings by Leon Chambers at The Soundhouse Ltd.